The First 100 Days

Obama in the Oval Office

Gregory Giroux
Congressional Quarterly (CQ Politics.com)

A Division of SAGE
Washington, D.C.

CQ Press
2300 N Street, NW, Suite 800
Washington, DC 20037

Phone: 202-729-1900; toll-free, 1-866-4CQ-PRESS (1-866-427-7737)

Web: www.cqpress.com

Cover design: Paula Goldstein
Composition: C&M Digitals (P) Ltd.
Image credits:
AP Images: 11, 16 (Clinton)
Getty: 1, 5, 6, 16 (Duncan, Geithner), 17 (Locke, Sebelius, Vilsack), 20, 23, 24, 25, 30, 32, 39
International Mapping Associates: 29
Newscom/CONGRESSIONAL QUARTERLY PHOTO BY SCOTT J. FERRELL: 17 (Solis)
Newscom/Digital Photo by ÂMark Reinstein-PHOTOlink: 17 (Salazar)
Newscom/UPI Photo/Roger L. Wollenberg: 16 (Donovan)
Reuters: 3, 7, 16 (Chu, Gates), 17 (Holder, Napolitano, Shinseki, LaHood)

♾The paper used in this publication exceeds the requirements of the American National Standard for Information Sciences—Permanence of Paper for Printed Library Materials, ANSI Z39.48-1992.

Printed and bound in the United States of America

13 12 11 10 09 1 2 3 4 5

ISBN 978-1-60426-601-6

Contents

OUTLINE:

- The First 100 Days: A Litmus Test?
- Swearing In and Inaugural Address
- Forming the Cabinet
- Role of Vice President Biden
- Executive Orders
- Shoring Up the Financial Industry
- Economic Stimulus Law
- Obama's "Unofficial" State of the Union
- Release of Fiscal 2010 Budget
- Omnibus Spending Bill
- Crisis in the U.S. Automobile Industry
- Foreign Policy
- Makeup of the New Congress
- Obama's First Bill Signing: Curbing Wage Discrimination
- Expansion of the Children's Health Insurance Program
- Environment and Energy
- Expanding National Service Programs
- D.C. Congressional Representation
- Delaying Transition from Analog to Digital TV
- Science Policy
- Swine Flu
- Senator Specter Switches Parties
- Administration's Use of Technology
- Public Opinion at 100 Days

President Obama talks on the telephone in the Oval Office on January 30, 2009, early in the first 100 days of his administration.

The First 100 Days: A Litmus Test?

Ever since Franklin D. Roosevelt became president seventy-six years ago, the 100-day marker has been used as a litmus test for evaluating early presidential accomplishment. Acting swiftly to assist a nation battered by the Great Depression, Roosevelt and an overwhelmingly Democratic-controlled Congress enacted fifteen pieces of legislation in his first 100 days. Political analysts and journalists ever since have applied the same 100-day metric to new presidents.

To be sure, 100 is an arbitrary benchmark. That short time period amounts to less than 7 percent of the number of days in a four-year presidential term. A new president spends much of that period making numerous appointments, and the legislative process doesn't always lend itself to speedy consideration of bills. Success in the first 100 days is no guarantee of success over an entire four-year term.

But 100 days is long enough to afford a glimpse into the priorities and decision-making style of a new administration. And the first 100 days of President Barack Obama's administration revealed stark differences between the new administration and the eight-year administration of his predecessor, Republican president George W. Bush, on domestic policy, foreign affairs, and the exercise of executive power.

Obama came to office facing more challenges at home and abroad than any president since Roosevelt. The nation was beset by a deep recession that included rising unemployment, huge federal budget deficits, and crises in the financial markets and U.S. automobile industry. The United States was in its seventh year fighting wars in Iraq and Afghanistan in which thousands of soldiers had died and that had drained the national treasury of hundreds of billions of dollars. Most Americans held a dim view about the direction of the country.

Obama sought early in his presidency to ameliorate these problems and assuage an uneasy public.

His first 100 days began with key reversals of Bush administration policies and ended with the passage of a $3.56 trillion budget blueprint that set a framework for Obama's spending priorities in the fiscal year that begins October 1, 2009. He called for beefed-up spending on health, education, the environment, and energy, among other initiatives. "This budget builds on the steps we've taken over the last 100 days to move this economy from recession to recovery and ultimately to prosperity," Obama said in a prime-time news conference held on April 29, his 100th day in office.

The president then ticked off a list of accomplishments early in his tenure: an economic stimulus law that he said "saved or created" over 150,000 jobs and provided a tax cut to 95 percent of working families; a reauthorization of a federal program (the Children's Health Insurance Program [CHIP], formerly known as SCHIP, the State Children's Health Insurance Program) to provide health insurance to children; and a financial industry rescue plan intended to thaw the frozen credit markets and curb home foreclosures. "So I think we're off to a good start, but it's just a start. I'm proud of what we've achieved, but I'm not content. I'm pleased with our progress, but I'm not satisfied," Obama said. "Millions of Americans are still without jobs and homes, and more will be lost before this recession is over. Credit is still not flowing nearly as freely as it should. Countless families and communities touched by our auto industry still face tough times ahead. Our projected long-term deficits are still too high, and government is still not as efficient as it needs to be."

The president continued: "We still confront threats ranging from terrorism to nuclear proliferation, as well as pandemic flu. And all this means you can expect an unrelenting, unyielding effort from this administration to strengthen our prosperity and our security in the second hundred days, in the third hundred days, and all of the days after that."

Obama's first 100 days didn't come without some embarrassing stumbles, though. Most notably, several of Obama's nominees for his cabinet had to withdraw from consideration because of personal tax troubles. And Obama had to confront a determined Republican opposition that maintained his fiscal policies spent too much federal money, increased the size and scope of the federal government, and didn't do enough to cut taxes.

President Obama addresses a news conference on April 29, 2009, his 100th day in office. Obama reassured Americans that they could expect "an unrelenting, unyielding effort from this administration to strengthen our prosperity and our security in the second hundred days, in the third hundred days, and all of the days after that."

"President Obama has inaugurated the most fiscally reckless administration in American history," Georgia representative Tom Price, the chairman of the conservative Republican Study Committee in the U.S. House, said on April 28. "The President has spent more money we don't have at a pace never imagined."

Still, most of the U.S. public viewed Obama favorably at the 100-day mark. According to a Gallup Poll taken between April 20 and April 26, Obama had an approval rating of 65 percent and a disapproval rating of 29 percent.[1] There was little fluctuation in Obama's approval ratings during his first 100 days as president.

This treatment will take a broad look at the first 100 days of the Obama administration, including the goals and policies Obama laid out in his inaugural address and in subsequent addresses to the American people; how he went about putting together his cabinet; how his early proposals were received in the Congress; and what the American public thought of his first 100 days as president.

Swearing In and Inaugural Address

Every four years, on January 20 of the year that follows a presidential election, a new or incumbent president takes the oath of office and delivers an inaugural address at a lavish ceremony attended by political luminaries and the public.

Gallup Daily: Obama Job Approval

Each result is based on a three-day rolling average

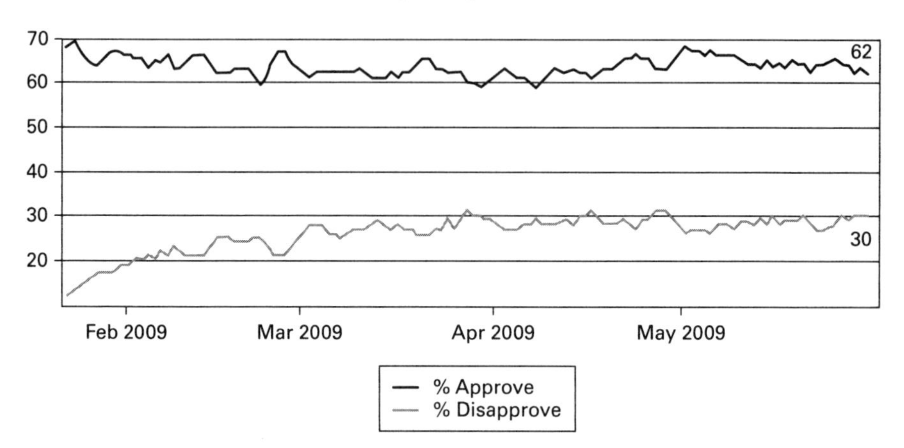

FIGURE 1
President Obama's Job Approval Ratings during the First Five Months

Source: http://sasorigin.onstreammedia.com/origin/gallupinc/GallupSpaces/Production/Cms/POLL/gde5fbrfc02zyjk0flujmg.gif. See also www.gallup.com/poll/113980/Gallup-Daily-Obama-Job-Approval.aspx.

More anticipation and significance attached to Obama's inauguration than others in recent history. In defeating Republican candidate John McCain for the presidency, Obama became the first black president in history and received nearly 70 million votes, more than any presidential candidate in history. And a record crowd convened in Washington, D.C., for the historic event: Obama's inauguration attracted an estimated 1.8 million attendees, almost certainly the largest attendance for any presidential inauguration and the largest crowd ever to gather on the capital's sprawling National Mall.[2]

There were some parallels between the inauguration of Obama and that of President Abraham Lincoln nearly 150 years earlier. Lincoln had been born 200 years earlier, in 1809, and is so closely identified with Illinois, Obama's home state, that the state is called the "Land of Lincoln." At the swearing-in ceremony, Obama's wife, Michelle, held the same Bible that was used for Lincoln's first inaugural in 1861. And like Lincoln, Obama ahead of his inauguration traveled to Washington by train along the East Coast.

In his inaugural address, Obama spoke of the many problems gripping the nation—among them war, a weak economy, and inefficiencies in education, health care, and energy. But he assured a restive nation that he would work to alleviate them.

"Today I say to you that the challenges we face are real. They are serious and they are many. They will not be met easily or in a short span of time. But know this, America: They will be met," Obama said.

EXCERPTS FROM PRESIDENT OBAMA'S INAUGURAL ADDRESS

January 20, 2009

"That we are in the midst of crisis is now well understood. Our nation is at war against a far-reaching network of violence and hatred. Our economy is badly weakened, a consequence of greed and irresponsibility on the part of some but also our collective failure to make hard choices and prepare the nation for a new age."

"Starting today, we must pick ourselves up, dust ourselves off, and begin again the work of remaking America."

"The question we ask today is not whether our government is too big or too small, but whether it works, whether it helps families find jobs at a decent wage, care they can afford, a retirement that is dignified. Where the answer is yes, we intend to move forward. Where the answer is no, programs will end."

"And for those who seek to advance their aims by inducing terror and slaughtering innocents, we say to you now that, 'Our spirit is stronger and cannot be broken. You cannot outlast us, and we will defeat you.'"

"To those who cling to power through corruption and deceit and the silencing of dissent, know that you are on the wrong side of history, but that we will extend a hand if you are willing to unclench your fist."

"What is required of us now is a new era of responsibility a recognition, on the part of every American, that we have duties to ourselves, our nation and the world, duties that we do not grudgingly accept but rather seize gladly, firm in the knowledge that there is nothing so satisfying to the spirit, so defining of our character than giving our all to a difficult task."

Huge crowds filled Washington, D.C.'s National Mall on January 20, 2009, to witness Obama's inauguration as the first African American president in U.S. history.

Obama delivers his inaugural address. He warned that "the challenges we face are real, they are serious and they are many" but that "they will be met."

The new president sought to strike the same bipartisan tones that he emphasized during his campaign. "On this day, we gather because we have chosen hope over fear, unity of purpose over conflict and discord," Obama said. "On this day, we come to proclaim an end to the petty grievances and false promises, the recriminations and worn out dogmas, that for far too long have strangled our politics."[3]

Obama called for "bold and swift" action to create new jobs and "lay a new foundation for growth" with improvements and innovations in infrastructure, science, health care, energy, and education. "Now, there are some who question the scale of our ambitions, who suggest that our system cannot tolerate too many big plans," Obama said. "Their memories are short, for they have forgotten what this country has already done, what free men and women can achieve when imagination is joined to common purpose, and necessity to courage."

On foreign policy, the new president reinforced his pledged to end the war in Iraq and also articulated support for human rights and civil liberties. "As for our common defense, we reject as false the choice between our safety and our ideals," Obama said.

The swearing-in ceremony even produced a few moments of awkwardness for Obama and Chief Justice John Roberts, who together fumbled the constitutionally prescribed oath of office.

In the recitation of the thirty-five-word pledge, it is customary for the chief justice to say, "I [name of president] do solemnly swear," which the president then repeats. As Roberts, who was reciting the oath from memory, was saying "do solemnly swear," Obama said, "I, Barack Hussein Obama."

Roberts then incorrectly recited the phrase "that I will faithfully execute the office of President of the United States" as "that I will execute the office of President to the United States faithfully." Obama initially paused, apparently waiting for Roberts to correct himself, then repeated Roberts's mistake of putting the word "faithfully" after "United States."

A second oath of office was administered the next day in the White House. Press Secretary Robert Gibbs said that the second oath was conducted out of an

Obama is given the presidential oath of office January 20, 2009, by Chief Justice John G. Roberts Jr. Obama's wife, Michelle, is holding the same Bible that President Abraham Lincoln used at his inauguration in 1861.

"abundance of caution"—a reference to the Constitution's prescription of a specific oath, with the word "faithfully" before the word "execute."[4]

Forming the Cabinet

One of the most important duties that a new president undertakes early in an administration is forming a cabinet—a collection of senior executive branch officials who manage large federal bureaucracies in their departments, promote the president's policy goals, and sometimes advise the president on policy matters.

Like past presidents, Obama began vetting cabinet members shortly after his election, and he introduced most of his selections before he was inaugurated so that his cabinet would be in place as he took office or shortly thereafter. A president's cabinet nominations are subject to hearings by a Senate committee and then a confirmation vote by the full Senate.

Secretary of State

Obama's choice for secretary of state, the nation' top diplomat, wasn't so controversial as it was surprising: New York senator Hillary Rodham Clinton, the former first lady who had battled Obama during their long campaign for the 2008 Democratic presidential nomination.

TIMELINE

OBAMA'S FIRST 100 DAYS

jan

20 Obama sworn in as president, delivers inaugural address.

22 Obama orders the closing of the Guantánamo Bay detention facility within one year.

29 Obama signs the Lilly Ledbetter Fair Pay Act of 2009.

feb

3 Former senator Tom Daschle, D-S.D., withdraws his nomination for secretary of health and human services.

9 Obama holds first press conference of his presidency.

12 Sen. Judd Gregg, R-N.H., withdraws his nomination for secretary of commerce.

13 Congress gives final approval to President Obama's economic recovery plan.

17 Obama signs the economic recovery bill into law.

24 Obama addresses a joint session of Congress to promote his economic programs.

26 Obama releases an outline for his budget for fiscal year 2010.

27 Obama says that U.S. combat troops will be out of Iraq by August 2010.

mar

9 Obama relaxes the Bush administration's restrictions on federal embryonic stem cell research.

27 Obama announces new administration policies on Afghanistan and Pakistan.

apr

12 Captain Richard Phillips rescued after U.S. Navy Seals kill his pirate captors southeast of Somalia.

13 Obama lifts most restrictions on travel to Cuba by Americans with family members there.

28 Pennsylvania senator Arlen Specter announces that he is switching his party affiliation from Republican to Democrat.

29 Congress gives final approval to a $3.56 trillion budget blueprint for fiscal year 2010.

Because she had been a rival of Obama's and wasn't an obvious choice for the secretary of state job, Clinton hadn't figured in the early cabinet speculation that always ensues after the election of a new president. But Clinton did offer strengths for the position, including prestige on the world stage and a familiarity with leaders that she had developed during her time in the Senate, where she served on the Foreign Relations Committee, and as first lady during the administration of her husband, President Bill Clinton.

"She's an American of tremendous stature who will have my complete confidence, who knows many of the world's leaders, who will command respect in every capital, and who will clearly have the ability to advance our interests around the world," Obama said on December 1, 2008, when he formally announced Clinton as his nominee.

Clinton's confirmation vote on January 21, 2009, was subject to a roll call vote rather than an uncontested voice vote because Texas Republican senator John Cornyn, the new chairman of the National Republican Senatorial Committee, had expressed some concerns over the measures that Clinton had promised to implement to guard against potential conflicts of interest involving foreign donations to former president Bill Clinton's foundation.

But Cornyn wound up voting to confirm Clinton, whose nomination was approved on a lopsided 94–2 vote. The only "no" votes came from Republicans Jim DeMint of South Carolina and David Vitter of Louisiana.[5]

Attorney General

For the job as the federal government's top prosecutor, Obama turned to Eric H. Holder Jr., a veteran Justice Department prosecutor who also headed the process of vetting Obama's potential vice-presidential candidates.

Holder's nomination drew opposition from Republican critics who said that he was hostile to gun owners' rights. Opponents also questioned whether Holder could discharge the duties of the office impartially, noting his role in some of President Clinton's controversial pardons and clemencies at the tail end of his administration.

But other Republicans joined Democrats in pronouncing Holder sufficiently well-qualified to serve as attorney general. The Senate confirmed him on February 2 by a vote of 75–21, including "yes" votes from nineteen of forty voting Republicans.[6]

Defense

Obama chose to retain Robert M. Gates, President Bush's second and final defense secretary, in his administration. Gates had served in the post since December 2006, when he succeeded Donald Rumsfeld, and previously served as director of the Central Intelligence Agency and on a bipartisan commission that studied the Iraq War.

In asking Gates to continue serving as defense secretary, Obama opted for continuity in a time of war. Obama was entering the White House in the first wartime presidential transition since 1969, when Republican Richard M. Nixon succeeded outgoing Democratic president Lyndon B. Johnson during the Vietnam War.

Obama said on December 1 that Gates "restored accountability" at the Pentagon and "won the confidence of military commanders, and the trust of our brave men and women in uniform, and their families."

Because Gates was the incumbent defense secretary, he did not have to be confirmed again by the Senate.

Transportation

For the post to oversee the nation's highway, aviation, railroad, and transit systems, Obama turned to a home-state colleague: Ray LaHood, a veteran U.S. House member from Illinois (1995–2009) who served six years on the Transportation and Infrastructure Committee.

Though LaHood didn't have a deep background in transportation policy, he did cultivate a reputation in Congress as a political centrist who promoted bipartisanship and civility.

"When I began this appointment process, I said I was committed to finding the best person for the job regardless of party," Obama said on December 19, 2008. "Ray's appointment reflects that bipartisan spirit, a spirit we need to reclaim in this country to make progress for the American people, and a spirit that Ray has embodied in all of his years in public service."

One of LaHood's tasks early in the Obama administration was to promote an economic stimulus law that spent billions of dollars on transportation infrastructure projects across the nation.

Commerce

In one of the Obama administration's biggest embarrassments during the first 100 days, it took three tries for the president to land a commerce secretary, who promotes economic growth and oversees the decennial census.

Obama's first choice was Bill Richardson, the New Mexico governor and a rival of Obama's for the 2008 Democratic presidential nomination. But Richardson withdrew from consideration on January 5, citing a grand jury investigation into whether state contracts that had been awarded to a firm were tied to its owner's large contributions to Richardson's campaigns.

Richardson denied wrongdoing, saying "unequivocally that I and my administration have acted properly in all matters and that this investigation will bear out that fact." Yet Richardson feared that the issue would have "forced an untenable delay in the confirmation process" and distracted from handling the economic crisis.

"As you might expect, I'm disappointed in the turn of events," Richardson said. "There were a lot of ways in which I thought I could help this country in a time of financial crisis. Sometimes your own dreams and plans must take a back seat to what is best for the nation."

Media reports suggested that Obama's aides pressured Richardson to step down and that the governor hadn't apprised the transition team about the seriousness of the investigation.

Obama on February 3 announced that he was nominating New Hampshire senator Judd Gregg, a moderately conservative Republican, as commerce secretary. It was a surprise choice, in part because of Gregg's party affiliation and in part because Gregg had voted more than a decade earlier for a budget bill that recommended shuttering the Commerce Department.[7]

But Gregg was respected and liked by Democratic and Republican senators. And Obama noted that while he and Gregg "don't agree on every issue," they did agree "on the urgent need to get American businesses and families back on their feet." "We see eye-to-eye on conducting the nation's business in a responsible, transparent and accountable manner," the president added.

But Gregg soon reconsidered his acceptance of Obama's offer, and he ultimately decided that it would be incompatible for him to serve in Obama's cabinet when he disagreed with some of the president's approaches to boosting the economy.

On February 12, nine days he was nominated, Gregg formally withdrew his name from consideration. He told reporters that "it just became clear to me that it would be very difficult, day in and day out, to serve in this cabinet or any cabinet, for that matter, and be part of a team and not be able to be 100 percent with the team, 110 percent with the team." Gregg also said that he would not seek reelection to the Senate in 2010.

"Once it became clear after his nomination that Senator Gregg was not going to be supporting some of President Obama's key economic priorities, it became necessary for Senator Gregg and the Obama administration to part ways," White House press secretary Robert Gibbs said.

On February 3, 2009, Obama introduces New Hampshire Republican senator Judd Gregg as his nominee for commerce secretary. Gregg withdrew his nomination nine days later, citing "irresolvable conflicts."

Barely twenty-four hours after he withdrew his nomination, Gregg voted against the Obama administration's economic stimulus measure on the grounds that it included "misplaced spending" and inadequate tax relief. Indeed, it would have been difficult for Gregg to serve as Commerce Secretary if he were opposing a major bill that his would-be boss backed to improve commerce and the economy.

On February 25, Obama nominated Gary Locke, the former Democratic governor of Washington State, for commerce secretary. Before describing Locke as "the right man for this job" and touting his background as a prosecutor, state representative, county executive, and governor, Obama noted that "I'm sure it's not lost on anyone that we've tried this a couple of times, but I'm a big believer in keeping at something until you get it right."

Locke expressed support for free-trade policies and tough enforcement of U.S. trade laws, and he assured senators that the Commerce Department would conduct an open and independent census. Locke's nomination on March 19 was unanimously approved, 25–0, by the Senate Commerce, Science and Transportation Committee. On March 24, more than two months after President Obama's inauguration, Locke was confirmed in an uncontested voice vote.[8]

Treasury

Obama's choice to head the Treasury Department was widely expected—Timothy F. Geithner, who had held senior positions at the department as well as at the World Bank and the New York Federal Reserve. Obama said that Geithner "offers not just extensive experience shaping economic policy and managing financial markets; he also has an unparalleled understanding of our current economic crisis in all of its depth, complexity and urgency."

But Geithner came under fire for his failure to pay thousands of dollars in Social Security and Medicare taxes when he was working at the International Monetary Fund earlier in the decade. Geithner, who immediately repaid the taxes, apologized repeatedly.

"These were careless mistakes. They were avoidable mistakes, but they were unintentional. I should have been more careful. I take full responsibility for them," Geithner said January 21 in an appearance before the Senate Finance Committee, which conducted his confirmation hearing.

Some senators were not assuaged. "If the man cannot handle his own finances, how is he going to handle the country's?" asked Iowa senator Charles E. Grassley, the top-ranking Republican on the Finance Committee.

A Rasmussen Reports poll showed that the public was essentially divided on whether Geithner should be named as Treasury secretary (though a majority of respondents also said that they were following the Geithner matter "not very closely" or "not at all.")[9]

But the tax issue didn't sink Geithner's nomination. Obama was foursquare behind this nomination, and he defended Geithner as the best possible person for the job at a time of financial turmoil.

The Senate Finance Committee on January 22 approved Geithner's nomination on an 18–5 vote, forwarding his nomination to the full Senate, which confirmed Geithner by a 60–34 vote six days later. The "no" votes came almost exclusively from Republicans, though three Democratic senators and one liberal independent senator also voted against Geithner's confirmation.[10]

Health and Human Services

Obama's first choice for this job was Tom Daschle, the former Senate majority leader from South Dakota. In nominating Daschle, who coauthored a book about overhauling health care, Obama said that he would also head a White House office of health care reform and would be the "lead architect" of the administration's health care policies.

But Daschle withdrew from consideration on February 3 after acknowledging that he failed to pay some taxes—mostly for the use of a car service—after he left the Senate following his defeat in the 2004 election. Daschle said that he did not want to detract from the Obama administration's efforts to enact a comprehensive health care overhaul. "The focus of Congress should be on the urgent business of moving the president's economic agenda forward, including affordable health care for every American," Daschle said in a joint statement with Obama, who said he accepted Daschle's decision "with sadness and regret."[11] Later that day, Obama told CNN journalist Anderson Cooper that he had "made a mistake" in the Daschle nomination. "I think I screwed up. And, you know, I take responsibility for it," Obama said.

Obama then turned to Kathleen Sebelius, the Democratic governor of Kansas, to fill the position of health and human services secretary (HHS). In formally announcing her nomination as HHS secretary on March 2, Obama said that Sebelius embodied "a commitment to bipartisan accomplishment" during her tenure as governor and previously as Kansas's insurance commissioner.

During the nomination process, Sebelius ran into trouble over her support for abortion rights and her ties to George Tiller, a Kansas abortion provider who had given money to Sebelius' political campaigns. (Tiller was shot to death on May 31, 2009, at his church in Wichita, Kansas.) Sebelius was forced to file an amended report to the Senate Finance Committee after an anti-abortion group revealed that Sebelius had understated her campaign support from Tiller.[12]

That speed bump wasn't enough to sink her nomination, though. On April 28, Sebelius was confirmed by a 65–31 vote, earning support from all voting Democrats and from nine Republican senators, including Sam Brownback and Pat Roberts of Kansas.[13]

Labor

Obama nominated Hilda L. Solis, a member of the U.S. House from southern California, to run the federal department that enforces laws relating to wage earners and their working conditions and employment opportunities. A daughter of immigrants from Mexico and Nicaragua who became naturalized American citizens, Solis was the first Hispanic woman chosen for Obama's cabinet.

Labor unions praised the nomination of Solis, who had backed increases in the federal minimum wage during her service in Congress. John Sweeney, the president of the AFL-CIO, said that he was "thrilled at the prospect of having Rep. Hilda Solis as our nation's next Labor Secretary."[14]

But Solis's confirmation was delayed after it was revealed that her husband had numerous tax liens against his business. Some critics pointed to her work as an uncompensated board member and former treasurer of the pro-union organization American Rights at Work. Anti-union activists also pointed to her support for the Employee Free Choice Act, a bill to ease union organizing that is commonly referred to as the "card check" bill and is strongly opposed by business groups.

These snags didn't derail Solis's confirmation. The Senate on February 24 approved Solis as labor secretary by an 80–17 vote, with all of the "no" votes coming from Republicans.[15]

Other Agencies

The rest of Obama's cabinet choices were not controversial, and all were confirmed without opposition. They are: Steven Chu, a Nobel Prize–winning physicist, to run the Energy Department; Shaun Donovan, New York City's housing director, to head the Department of Housing and Urban Development; Arne Duncan, the chief executive officer of the Chicago public school system, to run the Education Department; Janet Napolitano, the governor of Arizona, to head the Department of Homeland Security; Ken Salazar, a U.S. senator from Colorado, to be secretary of the interior; Eric Shinseki, a retired four-star army general and the army's former chief of staff, to be secretary of veterans affairs; and Tom Vilsack, a former Iowa governor who briefly competed with Obama for the 2008 Democratic presidential nomination, to be the agriculture secretary.

(For more background on Obama's cabinet, please see the box with thumbnail biographies of all cabinet members.)

Other Executive Branch Officials

Some other senior members are not officially members of the cabinet but have similar management and advisory functions. They include Christina Romer, an economist who heads the president's Council of Economic Advisers; Lisa P. Jackson, the administrator of the Environmental Protection Agency; Ron Kirk, the United States Trade Representative; Susan Rice, the U.S. ambassador to the United Nations; Peter R. Orszag, the director of the White House's Office of Management and Budget; Lawrence H. Summers, the director of the White House National Economic Council; and Rahm Emanuel, a former congressman from Chicago whom Obama selected to be White House chief of staff.

Obama also nominated Leon Panetta, a former U.S. House member from central California and a former chief of staff to President Bill Clinton, to head the Central Intelligence Agency (CIA). The announcement surprised even some Democratic senators, namely Intelligence Committee chair Dianne Feinstein of California, who said they hadn't been given a heads-up about Panetta's selection. Panetta's backers pointed to his executive experience in the Clinton White House and also said he would surround himself with intelligence professionals. The Senate on February 12 confirmed Panetta in an uncontested voice vote.[16]

Role of Vice President Biden

Obama's top adviser, and the first person in the presidential line of succession, is Vice President Joseph R. Biden Jr., who spent thirty-six years in the Senate representing Delaware and also rivaled Obama for the 2008 Democratic presidential nomination. The vice president serves as the president of the Senate, though the vice president almost never appears in the chamber except to break a tie vote.

In Obama's first 100 days, Biden emerged as a chief advocate of the administration's priorities on Capitol Hill and as a spokesman and diplomat on foreign policy matters. Both roles are natural fits for Biden, given his long service and friendships in the Senate, where he served as chairman of the Senate Foreign Relations Committee.

"My impression is that the president leans on him most heavily not just on his subjects of expertise, which are considerable, but on how you approach the House and Senate," Gregg said. "He's sort of like a senior counselor in many ways. He's the kind of person who's been around a while and seen it all and can give you good advice."[17]

Obama on January 30 tapped Biden to head a newly created Taskforce on Middle Class Working Families, which the president said would "bring together my economic advisers and members of my cabinet to focus on policies that will really benefit the middle class." The task force discussed issues such as making education and training opportunities more available and protecting retirement security. "With this task force, we have a single, highly visible group with one single goal: to raise the living standards of the people who are the backbone in this country: the middle class," Biden said.

During Obama's first 100 days, the task force met three times: on February 27 in Philadelphia, where it discussed ways to promote environmentally friendly "green jobs"; on March 19 in Washington, where it talked about how the economic recovery law helped middle-class families; and on April 17 in St. Louis, where the task force discussed ways to make college more affordable. In conjunction with each meeting, the task force released a lengthy report detailing its findings.

Biden also emerged as the White House's chief watchdog on implementation of the administration's economic recovery law. He frequently held conference calls with state and local officials to talk about how the measure was being implemented.

Biden on February 7 delivered the administration's first foreign policy address to an annual security conference in Munich, Germany. "We'll work in a partnership whenever we can, and alone only when we must. The threats we face have no respect for borders," Biden said.

Biden in March traveled to Brussels to exchange ideas with NATO allies about how to fight terrorist groups in Afghanistan and Pakistan.

Executive Orders

A president is granted the power to sign executive orders, which are proclamations that carry the force of law and can direct individuals or agencies to take specific actions without having to go through a cumbersome legislative process. While the Constitution doesn't expressly grant presidents the power to issue executive orders, the courts have generally upheld this power.

Obama issued some major executive orders in the first few days of his presidency.

Ethics

On January 21, Obama's first full day as president, he signed an executive order to impose stringent ethics commitments from executive branch staff. The order requires new staff to sign a pledge promising that they will not accept gifts from registered lobbyists or lobbying organizations. Executive agency appointees also cannot participate in any matters involving parties that are "directly or substantially related" to their former employers or clients.

Obama said that former lobbyists would not be allowed to "work on regulations or contracts directly and substantially related to their prior employer for two years."

"As I often said during the campaign, we need to make the White House the people's house, and we need to close the revolving door that lets lobbyists come into government freely and lets them use their time in public service as a way to promote their own interests over the interests of the American people when they leave," Obama said at a news conference shortly before signing the executive order.

Obama's ethics policy includes a "waiver" process to allow former lobbyists to serve in his administration, but critics have said it has been unevenly applied.

The Obama Cabinet

The cabinet is comprised of senior executive branch officials who advise the president on foreign and domestic policy. Cabinet officers are nominated by the president and then vetted by U.S. Senate in confirmation hearings and a vote.

A simple majority vote is needed to approve a cabinet nomination. Many cabinet officials are approved in a uncontested "voice vote."

President Obama's cabinet includes Vice President Joseph R. Biden Jr., who is first in the line of succession to the presidency, and the heads of fifteen executive departments. Those fifteen individuals are briefly profiled below.

Steven Chu, Energy
(www.energy.gov)
Confirmed January 20 by voice vote

Chu is a Nobel Prize–winning physicist who directed the Lawrence Berkeley National Laboratory in California. His background is in atomic particle physics.

Hillary Rodham Clinton, State
(www.state.gov)
Confirmed January 21 on a 94–2 vote

Clinton, a Yale-educated lawyer, was first lady from 1993 to 2001 and a U.S. senator from New York from 2001 until her confirmation. During her Senate tenure, Clinton was a member of the Foreign Relations Committee. She was Obama's chief rival for the 2008 Democratic presidential nomination.

Shaun Donovan, Housing and Urban Development
(www.hud.gov)
Confirmed January 22 by voice vote

Donovan was New York City's housing commissioner, a position he had held since 2004. During the Clinton administration, he was the deputy assistant secretary of multifamily housing at HUD.

Arne Duncan, Education
(www.ed.gov)
Confirmed January 20 by voice vote

Duncan was the chief executive officer of the public school system in Chicago, President Obama's hometown, from 2001 through 2008. He previously headed a nonprofit education foundation.

Robert M. Gates, Defense
(www.defenselink.mil)
Confirmed December 6, 2006, on a 95–2 vote

Gates was President Bush's second and final defense secretary, and Obama kept him on in his administration. Gates previously served as the director of the Central Intelligence Agency and as president of Texas A&M University.

Timothy F. Geithner, Treasury *(www.ustreas.gov)*
Confirmed January 26 on a 60–34 vote

Geithner was the head of the Federal Reserve Bank of New York and vice chairman of the committee that sets interest rates. He was Treasury's undersecretary for international affairs at the end of the Clinton administration and also worked at the International Monetary Fund.

Eric H. Holder Jr., Attorney General *(www.usdoj.gov)*

Confirmed February 2 on a 75–21 vote

Holder served as deputy attorney general during the Clinton administration. Clinton had previously tapped Holder to be the top federal prosecutor for the District of Columbia. In 1988, President Ronald Reagan made Holder a trial court judge in the nation's capital.

Ray LaHood, Transportation *(www.dot.gov)*

Confirmed January 22 by voice vote

LaHood, a Republican, represented the Peoria area and other areas of central Illinois in the U.S. House of Representatives (1995–2009). Prior to that he served for a decade as chief of staff to House Republican leader Robert H. Michel, whom LaHood succeeded in the House.

Gary Locke, Commerce *(www.commerce.gov)*

Confirmed March 24 by voice vote

Locke was a two-term governor of Washington State and the first Chinese American governor in U.S. history. He was the chief executive of King County (Seattle) and also served in the state legislature.

Janet Napolitano, Homeland Security *(www.dhs.gov)*

Confirmed January 20 by voice vote

Napolitano previously served as governor of Arizona, the state's attorney general, and as a federal prosecutor.

Ken Salazar, Interior *(www.doi.gov)*

Confirmed January 20 by voice vote

Salazar was a U.S. senator from Colorado (2005–2009) and previously served as the state's attorney general. Earlier in his career Salazar was the executive director of the Colorado Natural Resources Department.

Kathleen Sebelius, Health and Human Services *(www.hhs.gov)*

Confirmed April 28 on a 65–31 vote

Sebelius was twice elected as governor of Kansas and served from 2003 through her confirmation. She previously served as Kansas's insurance commissioner (1995–2003) and was a state legislator prior to that.

Eric Shinseki, Veterans Affairs *(www.va.gov)*

Confirmed January 20 by voice vote

Shinseki served as army chief of staff for four years, leaving in June 2003, just after the United States began waging military operations in Iraq. Shinseki told the Senate just before the war that it would take far more troops than planned. A decorated veteran of the Vietnam War, Shinseki is the first Asian American four-star general.

Hilda L. Solis, Labor *(www.dol.gov)*

Confirmed February 24 on a 80–17 vote

Solis represented southern California in the U.S. House from 2001 through her confirmation as labor secretary. She previously served in the California Assembly (1992–1994) and the California Senate (1994–2000).

Tom Vilsack, Agriculture *(www.usda.gov)*

Confirmed January 20 on a voice vote

Vilsack is a former two-term governor of Iowa (1999–2007). He sought the 2008 Democratic presidential nomination but withdrew before the primary and caucus voting began. He served in the Iowa Senate and was the mayor of Mount Pleasant prior to that.

Obama's choice for deputy secretary of defense, William Lynn, was a Raytheon Corporation lobbyist from 2002 to 2008 who would have been banned by Obama's ethics policy from serving in his administration. In a letter to the Obama administration, Iowa Republican senator Charles E. Grassley said that he "simply cannot comprehend how this particular lobbyist could be nominated to fill such a key position at DOD overseeing procurement matters, much less be granted a waiver from the ethical limitations listed in the Executive Order."[18]

Peter R. Orszag, the director of the Office of Management and Budget, and Gregory B. Craig, the counsel to the president, wrote a response letter to Grassley that said Lynn was well-qualified for the position and that "even the toughest rules . . . need reasonable exceptions."[19]

Orszag and Craig said that Lynn would divest his Raytheon stock within ninety days of his appointment and would not participate in decisions involving any of six specific Defense Department programs on which he had personally lobbied.

The Senate on February 11 confirmed Lynn on a 93–4 vote,[20] with the only "no" votes coming from Grassley; two other Republicans; and Missouri Democrat Claire McCaskill, who had said she was concerned about the Lynn nomination's "appearance of impropriety."[21]

Guantánamo Bay Prison

On January 22, Obama issued an executive order that ordered the closing, within one year, of the detainee facility operated by the Department of Defense in Guantánamo Bay, Cuba. Any detainees remaining in custody after one year will be sent home, released, or transferred to a third country or to another U.S. prison.

The Guantánamo Bay detention center had become an issue during the 2008 presidential campaign, with Obama saying that enemies of the United States were using the Guantánamo facility as a tool to recruit potential terrorists. Retired admiral Dennis Blair, Obama's choice to be director of national intelligence, said that the Guantánamo facility "has become a damaging symbol."

Republican lawmakers denounced the decision, saying that Americans would be much safer if suspected terrorists were held in the Cuba facility and not in the United States. House Republicans prepared legislation to bar federal courts from releasing Guantánamo detainees into the United States.

Interrogations

Obama signed a separate executive order directing that Guantánamo detainees must be treated in accordance with the Geneva Conventions, which forbids "humiliating and degrading" treatment. Obama required all agencies to limit themselves to interrogation techniques authorized in a September 2006 army field manual. The order effectively bars the use of "waterboarding," a kind of simulated drowning, and other harsh interrogation methods that detractors say are tantamount to torture.

Obama's executive order also barred the government from relying on any legal guidance the Bush administration issued after the September 11, 2001, terrorist attacks that isn't consistent with the new policies. "I can say without exception or equivocation that the United States will not torture," Obama said.[22]

"Mexico City" Abortion Policy

On January 23, Obama signed an executive order overturning a ban on providing assistance to any foreign, nongovernmental organization that performs abortions or promotes the practice as a method of family planning. Obama, a supporter of abortion rights, made the decision one day after the thirty-sixth anniversary of the *Roe v. Wade* Supreme Court case that legalized abortion rights.

Known as the "Mexico City Policy" because it was announced in that city by the Reagan administration at a United Nations population conference, the anti-abortion policy was rescinded in January 1993 by President Clinton, a supporter of abortion rights, and reinstated in January 2001 by President Bush, an opponent of abortion rights.[23]

Massachusetts Democratic senator John Kerry, the chairman of the Senate Foreign Relations Committee, said that he was "glad that President Obama has moved so swiftly to lift the global gag rule which has too long handcuffed our ability to provide aid around the world."[24] Abortion-rights and family planning groups also praised Obama's executive order.

Douglas Johnson, the legislative director for the National Right to Life Committee, an anti-abortion organization, described Obama's action as "the first in an anticipated series of attacks on long-standing pro-life policies, as the new administration pushes Obama's sweeping abortion agenda."[25]

Environment and Energy

Obama on January 26 signed an executive order directing the Department of Transportation (DOT) to establish higher fuel efficiency standards for carmakers' 2011 model year. He also directed the Environmental Protection Agency to review a proposal by California officials to set their own emissions standards above the national standard. The Bush administration in 2007 had denied California and thirteen other states a waiver from the national rules.

Stem Cell Research

Obama on March 9 issued an executive order that reversed restrictions that the Bush administration had placed on government funding of embryonic stem cell research.

Obama on March 9, 2009, signs an executive order relaxing the Bush administration's restrictions on the federal government's role in funding embryonic stem cell research. Obama said that while "the full promise of stem cell research remains unknown," scientists believe the research "may have the potential to help us understand and possibly cure some of our most devastating diseases and conditions."

Obama said that expanding embryonic stem cell research could help scientists better understand and possibly cure diseases such as Parkinson's and cancer and also help individuals with spinal cord injuries. "But that potential will not reveal itself on its own," Obama said. "Medical miracles do not happen simply by accident. They result from painstaking and costly research—from years of lonely trial and error, much of which never bears fruit—and from a government willing to support that work."

"When government fails to make these investments," the president added, "opportunities are missed."

Embryonic stem cell research is controversial because it involves destroying embryos to harvest the cells—a procedure that many religious conservatives liken to abortion. New Jersey representative Christopher H. Smith, a prominent anti-abortion legislator in Congress, said that "human-embryo-destroying stem cell research is not only unethical, unworkable and unreliable, it is now demonstrably unnecessary," pointing to advances in adult stem cell research.

Shoring Up the Financial Industry

The Obama administration moved early on a federal rescue of the financial markets, which had been disrupted by an explosion of "subprime" lending in the housing sector. Homebuyers took out these loans even though their incomes couldn't really afford them. Banks assumed these debts, and when the housing market faltered and people began defaulting on their mortgages, lenders sharply curtailed credit. The administration announced plans to bolster a $700 billion federal bank bailout program that had been enacted at the end of the Bush administration.

Treasury Secretary Timothy F. Geithner on February 10 said that the Obama administration's blueprint includes a "financial stability trust" to manage government investments in U.S. financial institutions. Major financial institutions were required to undergo a "stress test" to determine whether they have the capital necessary to continue lending. The administration's plan also imposed new requirements for banks to get federal aid. "The capital will come with conditions to help ensure that every dollar of assistance is used to generate a level of lending greater than what would have been possible in the absence of government support," Geithner said.

The administration's plan set up a public-private investment fund to use public financing to remove troubled assets, such as mortgage-backed securities, from institutions' balance sheets.

Geithner also said the administration would commit $50 billion to prevent home foreclosures and lower overall mortgage rates.

Economic Stimulus Law

Obama's signature legislative accomplishment in his first 100 days was to enact an economic recovery program to stimulate an economy that the president often said was in its worst crisis since the Great Depression.

According to the Commerce Department, the real gross domestic product—a key economic indicator that represents the output of goods and services produced by labor and property—decreased by 6.2 percent in the fourth quarter of 2008.[26] The Dow Jones Industrial Average, a prominent stock market index that measures the health of the nation's industrial sector, plunged throughout 2008 and early 2009; it reached an all-time low of 6,547 on March 9—the lowest total for the Dow in twelve years, and less than half the record high of 14,164 set on October 9, 2007.[27]

The U.S. House initiated action on an economic stimulus, passing a measure on January 28—just eight days after Obama was sworn in as president. The House's $819.5 billion measure called for $673.3 billion in estimated spending and $182.3 billion in net tax cuts to individuals and businesses over ten years. The 244–188 vote broke down mostly along party lines, with no Republicans voting for it and just eleven Democrats voting against it.[28]

Republicans said that the measure spent too much money and didn't include enough tax relief. They also groused that they were being shut out of the legislative process by House Democratic leaders that they said didn't abide by Obama's calls for bipartisanship.

The Senate initially considered an even more expensive economic stimulus plan, with a price tag of more than $900 billion. But the bill couldn't pass the Senate, which gives the minority party the power to filibuster or delay legislation, without the support from a group of political centrists who were concerned about the cost of the measure. So a group of Senate moderates in both parties hashed out a scaled-back version that would win the support of most Democrats and a few Republicans.

On February 10, the Senate passed its version of the bill that, at the request of the moderates, cut billions of dollars in spending programs. The key vote had occurred the day before, on February 9, on a cloture motion to limit debate on the bill. The motion succeeded, 61–36, with the support of all fifty-six voting Democrats, two liberal-leaning independents, and Republicans Olympia J. Snowe and Susan Collins of Maine and Arlen Specter of Pennsylvania.

One of the bill's most visible opponents was Arizona senator John McCain, whom Obama had defeated in the 2008 presidential election. McCain said that the package included excessive spending and amounted to "generational theft" because it would increase the federal debt. "What are we doing to future generations of Americans?" McCain said just ahead of the Senate approving the measure.[29]

The passage of separate bills by the House and Senate set the stage for a conference committee to come up with a compromise measure that both chambers would pass.

Obama, meanwhile, ventured outside the Beltway to promote an economic stimulus law as a necessary and urgent cure of the worst economy since the Great Depression.

"We have inherited an economic crisis as deep and as dire as any since the Great Depression. Economists from across the spectrum have warned that, if we don't act immediately, millions of more jobs will be lost," Obama said February 9 at a town hall meeting in Elkhart, Indiana, a top manufacturing center of recreational vehicles that had been hit hard by the recession. Obama said that the unemployment rate in Elkhart had risen to more than 15 percent from 4.7 percent just a year earlier.

Absent congressional action to aid the economy, Obama warned in stark terms, "the national unemployment rates will approach double digits, not just here in Elkhart, all across the country. More people will lose their homes and their health care. And our nation will sink into a crisis that at some point we may be unable to reverse."

On February 12 Obama appeared in the Peoria area, a traditional barometer of Middle America. "Well, you notice I've been traveling a little bit," Obama said at a Caterpillar plant. "I had to come to Peoria. You have to see how things are playing in Peoria."

Obama said that his economic recovery package would help companies like Caterpillar, which produces construction and mining equipment. Obama said February 11 that his plan would allow Caterpillar to rehire some laid-off workers,[30] though Caterpillar CEO Jim Owens said after the president's appearance that he was more likely to lay off additional employees before he would rehire some of those who had already lost their jobs.[31]

House and Senate negotiators produced a conference report late in the evening of February 12. The agreement called for $789.5 billion in spending and tax cuts—$29.5 billion less than the House bill and $48.5 billion less than the Senate version.[32] Its spending provisions include an extension of unemployment and welfare benefits, Medicaid benefits to states, and grants for health information technology. It also

Obama delivers a speech on the economy and touts his economic recovery plan on February 12, 2009, at an East Peoria, Illinois, Caterpillar plant that shed jobs during the national recession.

increased grants for state and local schools and funds for public housing, transportation, and nutrition assistance.

Obama and most Democrats had to agree to cut some spending to secure the backing of Senators Snowe, Collins, and Specter, whose votes were crucial to the bill's enactment. Some House liberals said that they wanted to see more federal spending in the measure.

On the tax side, the agreement extended current accelerated depreciation allowances for businesses, suspended taxes on the first $2,400 of unemployment benefits for 2009, and expanded other individual tax credits.

House Republican leaders denounced the conference agreement as too much federal spending and not enough in tax relief. They also groused that the conference report became available at 11:00 p.m., the night before the final vote. This, Republicans said, ran counter to Democratic leaders' initial promises that the 111th Congress would be the most transparent in history.

"What's in it? Have you read it?" Georgia representative Tom Price, a leader of Republican conservatives in the U.S. House, said during House debate on February 13 as he brandished a copy of the thousand-page document.

The House cleared the measure on February 13 by a vote of 246–183. Once again, no Republican voted for the measure, which secured the support of all but seven Democrats. (One Democrat, Daniel Lipinski of Illinois, voted "present" on final passage.)

Vice President Joseph R. Biden Jr. watches Obama on February 17, 2009, sign his economic recovery plan into law at a ceremony in Denver, Colorado, the same city where Obama six months earlier formally accepted the 2008 Democratic presidential nomination.

Hours later, the Senate voted, 60–38, to waive objections to the conference report—a move that required a sixty-vote majority—and paved the way for the Senate to clear the bill in an uncontested voice vote.[33]

It actually took more than five hours for the Senate to reach that sixty-vote threshold, in part, because just three Republican senators supported the measure and Massachusetts Democrat Edward M. Kennedy, suffering from brain cancer, was too ill to participate in the vote. So Democratic leaders kept the roll call going late into the evening so that Democrat Sherrod Brown could fly back to Washington from Ohio, where he was attending a memorial service for his late mother.

Obama signed the bill on February 17 in Denver, where he had accepted the Democratic presidential nomination at his party's convention less than six months earlier. The measure is the "most sweeping economic recovery package in our history," Obama said.

"Now, I don't want to pretend that today marks the end of our economic problems, nor does it constitute all of what we're going to have to do to turn our economy around," Obama said. "But today does mark the beginning of the end; the beginning of what we need to do to create jobs for Americans scrambling in the wake of lay-offs; the beginning of what we need to do to provide relief for families worried that they won't be able to pay next month's bills; the beginnings of the first steps to set our economy on a firmer foundation, paving the way to long-term growth and prosperity."

Obama's "Unofficial" State of the Union

On February 24, one week after Obama signed the economic stimulus plan into law, he addressed a joint session of the House of Representatives and the Senate to promote his policy agenda for the coming year.

Obama's address was technically not a "State of the Union" speech, which a president delivers after his first full year in office. But it otherwise looked like one: the

Obama on February 24, 2009, delivers his first address to a joint session of Congress. "What is required now is for this country to pull together, confront boldly the challenges we face, and take responsibility for our future once more," he said.

vice president and the Speaker sat in the two chairs behind and above the president, and the televised speech was followed by a televised response by a leading member of the opposition political party.

Obama's speech reminded listeners that "for many Americans watching right now, the state of our economy is a concern that rises above all others."

"But while our economy may be weakened and our confidence shaken; though we are living through difficult and uncertain times, tonight I want every American to know this: We will rebuild, we will recover, and the United States of America will emerge stronger than before," the president said.

Obama touted his just-signed economic stimulus law and laid out an ambitious legislative program on a wide variety of issues. He called for legislation to promote the flow of credit, shore up troubled banks and save the domestic automakers.

On energy, the president called for using clean, renewable sources of energy to help make the country energy independent.

He called for overhauling the health care system to hold down costs and cover more people with insurance.

On education, Obama called for improvements to the education system so that the U.S. workforce can be prepared for the global economy. The goal of his administration, he said, is to "ensure that every child has access to a complete and competitive education."

"None of this will come without cost, nor will it be easy," Obama said. "But this is America. We don't do what's easy. We do what's necessary to move this country forward."

Release of Fiscal 2010 Budget

One of the most consequential actions that a president and the Congress undertake every year is the putting together and passing of a budget. This process takes up a good part of the year, beginning with the president's submission of a budget to the Congress in the early part of the year.

On February 26, Obama administration officials released the broad outlines of a $3.55 trillion budget for fiscal year 2010, which begins October 1, 2009, and ends September 30, 2010.

Obama's budget shows the deficit soaring this year before falling in subsequent years. The fiscal 2009 deficit will be $1.8 trillion, according to the budget, easing to $1.2 trillion in fiscal 2010 and $533 billion in fiscal 2013.

His budget outline called for creating a $634 billion "reserve fund" to start expanding health care coverage to more Americans. About half of the cost of the health program would come from savings in Medicare and Medicaid programs.

Obama's budget proposal also called for increased spending on education, environmental, and energy programs. It proposed creating a "cap-and-trade" system to regulate carbon emissions that would raise $646 billion in revenues, of which $120 billion would be used for renewable energy programs.

His budget called for limiting the itemized deductions that upper-income taxpayers can claim, as well as allowing for the expiration of tax cuts for upper-income taxpayers that were included in measures President Bush signed into law in 2001 and 2003.

"While we must add to our deficits in the short term to provide immediate relief to families and get our economy moving, it is only by restoring fiscal discipline over the long run that we can produce sustained growth and shared prosperity," Obama said.

Republicans criticized Obama's budget, saying constantly that it "spends too much, taxes too much and borrows too much."

Congress spent much of March and April considering the non-binding budget resolutions that set how much money that appropriators can spend. After the House and Senate passed slightly different budget resolutions, the two chambers agreed on a compromise bill that called for total spending of $3.5 trillion in fiscal year 2010, slightly less than Obama had proposed. The measure included instructions that would allow Obama's health care overhaul to move through Congress without being subject to a filibuster in the Senate.

The House passed the budget agreement on April 29, Obama's 100th day in office, by a near party-line vote of 233–193; later in the day, the Senate passed it on a 53–43 vote.

Omnibus Spending Bill

President Obama on March 11 signed into law a catch-all appropriations bill that spent $410 billion on a variety of domestic and State Department programs for the remainder of fiscal year 2009 (which began October 1, 2008, and will end September 30, 2009). The measure was called an "omnibus" appropriations bill because it rolled together nine spending bills that were never enacted.

The bill included spending increases that Democrats sought in 2008 but that President Bush opposed as too costly. So instead of trying to pass a bill that Bush would veto, Democratic leaders agreed to pass a "continuing resolution" that spent money at existing levels. That resolution was set to expire on March 6.

With Obama more sympathetic than Bush to increased federal spending, House Democratic leaders promoted a beefed-up omnibus bill and passed it on February 25. But it became hung up in the Senate, where Republicans demanded amendments be added to the measure, and so Congress instead passed another continuing resolution to keep the government operating through March 11.

The Senate cleared the measure for Obama's signature on March 10 in an uncontested voice vote after first agreeing, on a 62–35 vote, to end debate on the bill. Republicans urged Obama to veto the omnibus bill, in part because it included thousands of "earmarks," the narrowly tailored spending programs that members of Congress seek for district projects. The nonpartisan group Taxpayers for Common Sense said that the measure included more than 8,500 earmarks totaling $7.7 billion.[34]

Obama described the bill as "imperfect" but said he was signing it "because it is necessary for the ongoing functions of government."[35]

Crisis in the U.S. Automobile Industry

One of the biggest challenges for Obama is how to revitalize the domestic automobile industry, which in recent years has been hurt by the rising price of oil and by high labor costs. In Michigan, the heart of the U.S. domestic automobile industry, the unemployment rate in early 2009 reached 10 percent, the highest joblessness rate in the nation.

At the tail end of 2008, before Obama took office, President Bush signed a bill to provide General Motors (GM) and Chrysler with emergency loans on the grounds that they would submit proposals to restructure their operations. (Ford Motor Corporation, the other of the "Big Three" auto manufacturers, did not receive federal funds.)

Under the terms of the loans, GM and Chrysler had to submit initial long-term restructuring plans by February 17 and then final plans by March 31. Their initial plans requested more government assistance and outlined some job reductions.

"Everybody's gonna have to come to the table and say it's important for us to take serious restructuring steps now in order to preserve a brighter future down the road," Obama said March 29 on the CBS news program *Face the Nation*.

On March 30, the Obama administration at its request received the resignation of GM chairman and chief executive officer Rick Wagoner. The administration also said that additional federal aid to Chrysler, which is in worse shape than GM, would be contingent on Chrysler merging successfully with the Italian automaker Fiat.

Obama gave GM sixty days and Chrysler thirty days to submit new restructuring plans. "During this period, they must produce plans that would give the American people confidence in their long-term prospects for success," Obama said. "And what we're asking for is difficult. It will require hard choices by companies. It will require unions and workers who've already made extraordinarily painful concessions to do more. It will require creditors to recognize that they can't hold out on for the prospect of endless government bailouts. It will require efforts from a whole host of other stakeholders including dealers and suppliers."

"Only then," the president said, "can we ask American taxpayers who've already put up so much of their hard-earned money to once more invest in a revitalized auto industry."

On March 31, the day after Obama's announcement, interim GM CEO Fritz Henderson, a twenty-five-year veteran of the company, said at a news conference that he hoped to restructure the company without having to file for bankruptcy to eliminate some debts, but that court action was "more probable." On June 1 GM filed for Chapter 11 bankruptcy, and the federal government took a 60 percent ownership stake in the troubled company.

Foreign Policy

Though the economic crisis dominated the attention of most Americans, Obama had to grapple with numerous global flash points at the beginning of his presidency.

On January 22, his second full day in office, Obama appeared at the State Department headquarters on Hillary Rodham Clinton's first full day as secretary of state. The two former rivals for the presidency announced a pair of special envoys to forge peace in some global hotspots—Richard Holbrooke to Afghanistan and Pakistan, the central front in the U.S. campaign against terrorism, and George J. Mitchell to the Middle East, to deal with the conflagration in the Gaza Strip between Israel and the Islamic militant group Hamas.

Obama described Holbrooke, a former U.S. ambassador to the United Nations, as "one of the most talented diplomats of his generation." The president said that Mitchell, a former Senate majority leader from Maine who helped forge a peace agreement in Ireland in the 1990s, was "renowned in this country and around the world for his negotiating skill."

Obama on January 26 gave his first formal interview as president to the Dubai-based Al-Arabiya Network. "My job to the Muslim world is to communicate that the Americans are not your enemy," Obama said.

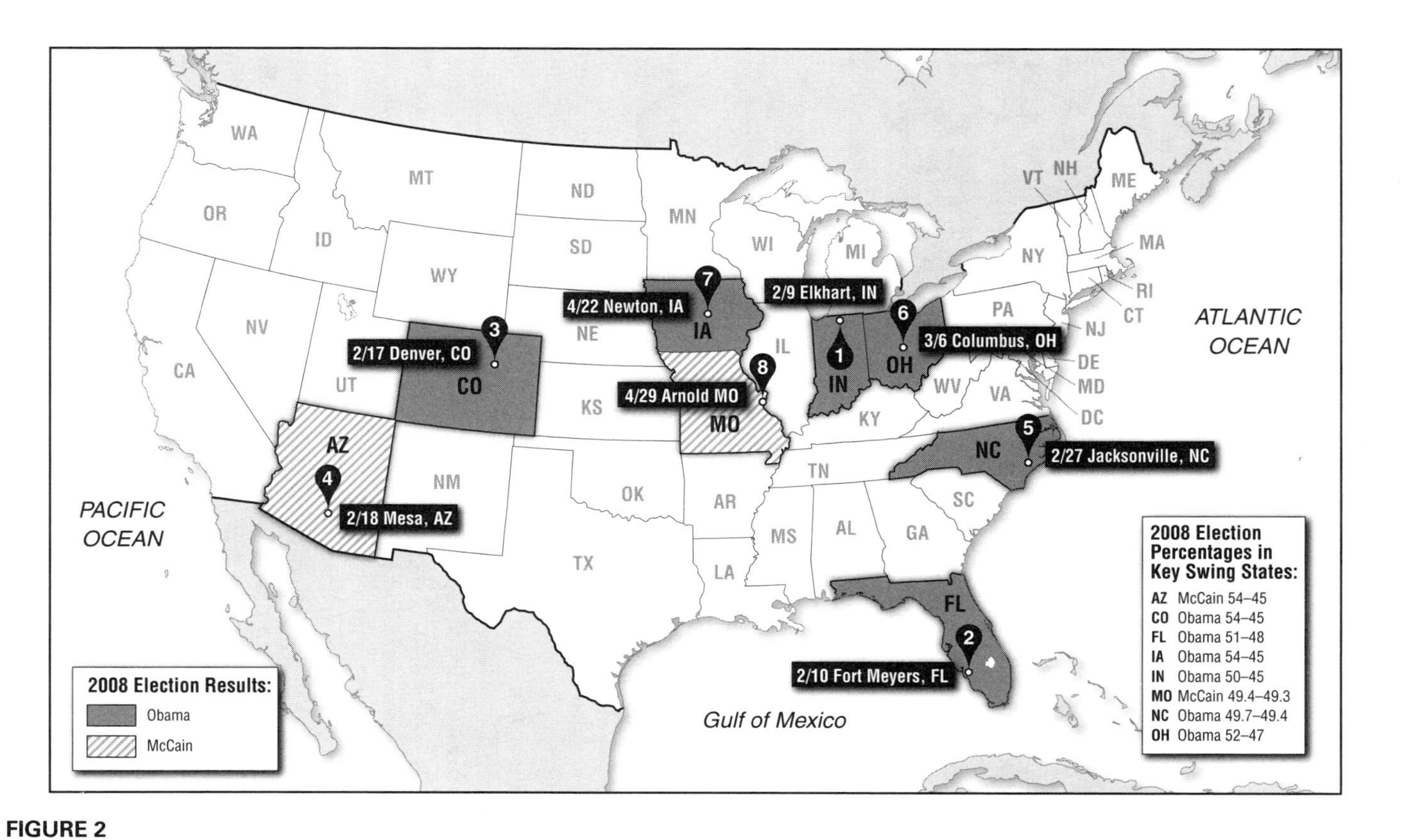

FIGURE 2
Swing States Visited by Obama in His First 100 Days

Source: Data compiled by author.

On April 3, 2009, Obama participates in a "town hall"–style meeting in Strasbourg, France, one of the cities hosting a North Atlantic Treaty Organization (NATO) summit.

On February 19, Obama made his first foreign trip as president to Canada, where he met with Prime Minister Stephen Harper in Ottawa to talk about trade and other issues of importance to the neighboring countries.

Obama said that he made the trip to "to underscore the closeness and importance of the relationship between our two nations and to reaffirm the commitment of the United States to work with friends and partners to meet the common challenges of our time."

Obama in early March welcomed Gordon Brown, the prime minister of the United Kingdom, to Washington, D.C., to talk about ways the two nations could ease the global financial crisis. In an address to a joint meeting of Congress on March 4, Brown hailed the close relationship between the United States and Britain.

Later in the month, in his first major trip overseas as president, Obama traveled to London to meet with Brown and other world leaders who were in the British capital for the G-20 Leaders' Summit on Financial Markets and the World Economy. The world leaders talked about ways their countries could curb the global financial crisis.

Later in that trip, Obama appeared at a "town hall" meeting in Strasbourg, France, to promote a long-term goal of ridding the world of nuclear weapons. "Even with the Cold War now over, the spread of nuclear weapons or the theft of nuclear material could lead to the extermination of any city on the planet," Obama said.

He outlined more details of his strategy in a speech in Prague. Obama said on April 5 that the United States and Russia would negotiate a new Strategic Arms Reduction Treaty. The president also said that his administration would "immediately and aggressively" pursue U.S. ratification of the Comprehensive Test Ban Treaty, under which signatories agree not to carry out any nuclear weapon test explosion or any other nuclear explosion.

"It is only by coordinating with countries around the world that we will stop the spread of the world's most dangerous weapons," Obama said in his weekly radio address on April 11.

Iraq

Obama's 2008 campaign was aided by his promise to end the long U.S. war in Iraq, which the Congress had authorized the Bush administration to undertake in late 2002. Though the Iraq war in early 2009 had waned in significance in the minds of voters—economic concerns had become paramount and the success of a U.S. troop "surge" had significantly reduced violence in Iraq—Obama was intent on ending the U.S. presence in Iraq, if on a less aggressive timetable than he promoted during the campaign.

On February 27, Obama said at the Marine Corps base in Camp Lejeune, North Carolina, that the United States "will pursue a new strategy to end the war in Iraq through a transition to full Iraqi responsibility."

"Let me say this as plainly as I can: by August 31, 2010, our combat mission in Iraq will end," Obama said.

The president said that the United States would retain a "transitional force" after that date to help train, equip, and advise Iraqi security forces and also conduct targeted counterterrorism missions. Obama said this U.S. presence would consist of between 35,000 and 50,000 troops who would gradually redeploy out of Iraq by the end of 2011.

"The drawdown of our military should send a clear signal that Iraq's future is now its own responsibility," Obama said. "The long-term success of the Iraqi nation will depend on decisions made by Iraq's leaders and the fortitude of the Iraqi people."

Obama also announced a beefed-up diplomatic effort headed up by Christopher R. Hill, a veteran diplomat whom the president tapped as the new U.S. ambassador to Iraq. The U.S. Senate confirmed Hill for the post on April 21 by a vote of 73–23.[36]

Obama's plan drew praise from Democrats and Republicans alike—including John McCain, his rival for the presidency.

"Given the gains in Iraq and the requirements to send additional troops to Afghanistan, together with the significant number of troops that will remain in Iraq and the president's willingness to reassess based on conditions on the ground, I am cautiously optimistic that the plan as laid out by the president can lead to success," McCain said.[37]

Obama on April 7 made a surprise trip to Iraq to thank the troops for their service and also meet with the commanding officers in the nation. "We've made significant political progress. You've seen a greater willingness on the part of all the factions in Iraq to resolve their issues politically and through non-violent means," Obama said.

Obama greets U.S. troops during a surprise visit to Baghdad, Iraq, on April 7, 2009. The president also met with Gen. Ray Odierno, the U.S. military commander in Iraq, as well as with Iraqi prime minister Nouri al-Maliki.

Afghanistan and Pakistan

Obama on March 27 announced new plans for Afghanistan and Pakistan to target al-Qaeda terrorists that are using those nations' mountainous terrains as "safe havens" to hide, train terrorists, and plot new attacks.

The president announced new military, diplomatic, and development initiatives, including a deployment of 4,000 U.S. troops to train Afghan security forces so that they can "take responsibility for their country." Obama, who had earlier announced a deployment of 17,000 troops to Afghanistan, set a goal of building an Afghan army of 134,000 and a police force of 82,000 by 2011.

The president also called for a beefed-up civilian effort in Afghanistan, which has been plagued by a large narcotics trade and corruption in government. He said that agricultural specialists, educators, engineers, and lawyers were needed to "help the Afghan government serve its people and develop an economy that isn't dominated by illicit drugs."

Obama called on Congress to pass a bill, sponsored by Democratic senator John Kerry of Massachusetts and Republican senator Richard G. Lugar of Indiana, to authorize $1.5 billion in nonmilitary assistance to Pakistan over five years.

Cuba

The Obama administration said April 13 that it would lift most restrictions on travel to Cuba by Americans who have family members in that island country, which Fidel Castro has ruled for most of the past half-century. The Obama administration also authorized U.S. telecommunications companies to establish fiber-optic and satellite connections with Cuba and authorized the export of some humanitarian goods.

"All who embrace core democratic values long for a Cuba that respects the basic human, political and economic rights of all of its citizens," White House press secretary Robert Gibbs said. "President Obama believes the measure he has taken today, will help make that goal a reality."

But Florida Republican representative Lincoln Diaz-Balart, whose congressional district in southeastern Florida includes a large concentration of Cuban Americans, said that Obama's decision was a "serious mistake" that would help the Castro regime.

Makeup of the New Congress

Obama's agenda would have faced bigger hurdles had it not been aided by a Congress with large Democratic Party majorities in both the House and the Senate. The 111th Congress convened January 6 with 256 Democrats and 178 Republicans in the House. (There was one vacancy, in the Chicago-centered and strongly Democratic district that Rahm Emanuel vacated to become Obama's chief of staff.) In the 2008 elections, the Democrats made a net gain of three seats in special elections in the spring and netted another twenty-one seats in the regular fall elections. The 256 seats are the most that the Democrats have held in fifteen years.

In the Senate, Democrats effectively controlled fifty-eight seats, including those of liberal-leaning independents Joseph I. Lieberman of Connecticut and Bernard Sanders of Virginia, and the Republicans controlled forty-one seats. One Senate seat in Minnesota was vacant because there had been no confirmed winner in the November 2008 race between Republican incumbent Norm Coleman and Democratic challenger Al Franken. A recount of votes in early 2009 gave Franken a small edge, but Coleman contested the result in court and the case dragged on for months.

The Democratic Party maintained its 58–41 advantage in the Senate even after Obama and Biden resigned their seats to enter the White House. The Democratic governors in Illinois and Delaware appointed Democratic successors, ensuring that there would be no change in the partisan balance of the Senate.

Obama was succeeded by Roland W. Burris, a former Illinois state attorney general who was appointed in controversial fashion by Democratic governor Rod R. Blagojevich three weeks after Blagojevich's December 9 arrest on federal corruption charges—including an allegation that the governor sought to trade the Senate seat for personal enrichment and campaign contributions. Burris denied any quid pro quo arrangement with Blagojevich, but the controversy surrounding the appointment was an early distraction for Obama.

Biden was succeeded by Ted Kaufman, his former Senate chief of staff. Kaufman said that he would not run in a 2010 special election to serve the remaining four years of the term that Biden had won in 2008. It's widely expected that Biden's eldest son,

Democratic state attorney general Beau Biden, will run for the Senate seat long held by his father.

Two other Democratic senators resigned to join the Obama administration—Hillary Rodham Clinton of New York, who became secretary of state, and Ken Salazar of Colorado, who became interior secretary. The Democratic governors in those states appointed Kirsten Gillibrand, a member of the U.S. House from upstate New York, and Michael Bennet, the superintendent of the public schools in Denver.

The Democrats later secured a fifty-ninth Senate seat after Pennsylvania Republican senator Arlen Specter announced April 28 that he would switch to the Democratic Party. Should Franken ultimately be seated in Minnesota, the Democrats would have sixty Senate seats—theoretically enough to achieve the three-fifths supermajority vote needed to break filibusters lodged by the minority party.

Gillibrand's elevation to the Senate required her to resign her seat in the U.S. House, setting in motion a special election on March 31 to determine her successor in New York's 20th District, a mostly rural and exurban area near Albany.

Republicans had hoped to make the race an early referendum on the Obama administration. Though Obama had narrowly defeated John McCain in New York's 20th District in the 2008 election, the race initially appeared to be the Republicans' to lose because their candidate, state assembly minority leader James Tedisco, was a veteran legislator and well known in the district. Democratic nominee Scott Murphy was a businessman who had never before run for public office.

Yet Murphy sliced into Tedisco's big early lead in polls, in part because he emphasized his support for Obama's economic stimulus law. Tedisco initially didn't say how he would have voted, though he later came out in opposition to the measure.

The Democratic National Committee aired a television ad that highlighted Obama's endorsement of Murphy, heightening the national significance of the contest. Both major political parties spent hundreds of thousands of dollars on the race, in addition to the nearly $4 million that Tedisco and Murphy together spent on the contest.

The tally on election night was so close that Murphy didn't emerge as the winner until after a weeks-long count of thousands of absentee ballots. Tedisco conceded the race on April 24, after a nearly complete count of votes put Murphy ahead by about 400 votes out of more than 160,000 cast.

Obama's First Bill Signing: Curbing Wage Discrimination

With significant majorities in both chambers of Congress, Democrats were prepared to clear legislation to be signed by President Obama—rather than vetoed by President Bush.

Obama signed his first bill into law on January 26, a measure that will make it easier for employees to bring wage discrimination suits.

The law reversed a 2007 Supreme Court decision, *Ledbetter v. Goodyear Tire & Rubber Co.*, that said that workers suing for pay restitution had to do so within 180 days of the first discriminatory paycheck. Lilly Ledbetter, for whom the new law was named, had discovered after twenty years of employment that she was getting paid less than her male colleagues for equal work.

The bill amended the statute of limitations to apply to each discriminatory paycheck or action.

Republican opponents said that the bill would invite a rash of lawsuits, but Democrats said that it would restore the law to what it was before the 2007 Supreme Court case.

It had stalled in the Senate in the 110th Congress (2007–2008), but the larger Democratic majorities in the 111th Congress put the measure on a trajectory of passage.

The Senate passed the measure on January 22 by a vote of 61–36, with all fifty-four voting Democrats joining two Democratic-aligned independents and five Republicans in voting for it. The five Republican "aye" votes included Pennsylvania senator Arlen Specter and the four Republican senators who are women: Lisa Murkowski of Alaska; Kay Bailey Hutchison of Texas; and Susan Collins and Olympia J. Snowe of Maine.[38]

Five days later, on January 27, the U.S. House of Representatives passed the measure by a vote of 250–177, thus clearing the bill for President Obama's signature. As in the Senate, the House vote broke heavily along party lines: three Republicans voted "aye" and five Democrats voted "no."[39]

Obama signed the bill into law at a January 29 ceremony that included Ledbetter, whom the president said "set out on a journey that would take more than ten years, take her all the way to the Supreme Court, and lead to this bill which will help others get the justice she was denied." The president later said that "in signing this bill today, I intend to send a clear message: That making our economy work means making sure it works for everyone. That there are no second class citizens in our workplaces, and that it's not just unfair and illegal—but bad for business—to pay someone less because of their gender, age, race, ethnicity, religion or disability."

Expansion of the Children's Health Insurance Program

Another early priority of the Obama administration and its Democratic congressional allies was a reauthorization and expansion of the Children's Health Insurance Program—better known by the acronym CHIP.

CHIP, first enacted in 1997 (when it was called the State Children's Health Insurance Program, or SCHIP), was designed to assist the children of working parents who made too much to qualify for Medicaid but not enough to afford expensive private insurance. About 29 million children are enrolled in Medicaid and 7 million in CHIP.[40]

The Democratic-run 110th Congress (2007–2008) had passed a SCHIP expansion, only to see it twice vetoed by President Bush on the grounds that it was too expensive. With a pro-expansion president in office, the measure wasn't all that difficult to pass early in the 111th Congress.

The Senate on January 29 passed a four-and-one-half-year, $32.8 billion CHIP expansion by a vote of 66–32, with nine Republicans joining fifty-five Democrats and two independents in voting "aye." The "no" votes came exclusively from Republicans.[41]

On February 4, the House cleared the measure for President Obama's signature by a vote of 290–135. Forty Republicans voted for it and just two Democrats voted against it.

President Obama signed the bill into law later that day, saying that in doing so "we fulfill one of the highest responsibilities that we have: to ensure the health and well-being of our nation's children." "It's a responsibility that's only grown more urgent as our economic crisis deepens, as health care costs have exploded and millions of families are unable to afford health insurance," Obama elaborated.

But the president made clear that an expansion of the children's health insurance programs was but a first step toward a larger goal of universal health coverage. "Because the way I see it," Obama said, "providing coverage to 11 million children through CHIP is a down payment on my commitment to cover every single American."

Environment and Energy

Obama touted a number of provisions in the economic stimulus law that he said would promote energy efficiency: modernizing federal buildings to save energy costs; providing grants to states to weatherize homes; and providing tax credits for consumers who purchase more energy-efficient cooling and heating systems.

Shortly before he signed the economic stimulus law, Obama sent a memorandum to the Department of Energy directing the agency to finalize energy efficiency standards for a range of residential and commercial products, like dishwashers and refrigerators.[42]

"We are already seeing reports from across the country of how this is beginning to create jobs, as local governments and businesses rush to hire folks to do the work of building and installing these energy efficient products," Obama said April 22 in Newton, Iowa. "And these steps will spur job creation and innovation as more Americans make purchases that place a premium on reducing energy consumption."

Expanding National Service Programs

Obama on April 21 signed into law a measure to expand national and community service programs like AmeriCorps. The new law, which was passed with overwhelming bipartisan majorities in both the House and the Senate, was named to honor Massachusetts senator Edward M. Kennedy, who had sponsored the measure in the Senate.

The new law, which has an estimated cost of $5.7 billion over five years, expands the mission of the Corporation for National and Community Service to provide more incentives for students and senior citizens to participate in community service projects. It would also increase, from $4,725 to $5,350, the education reward for volunteers and tie future increases to the maximum Pell grant.[43]

D.C. Congressional Representation

Advocates of full congressional representation for the District of Columbia had hoped that Obama's election and the expanded Democratic majorities in Congress would pave the way for the national capital to have a full-fledged member of Congress. The District of Columbia has a congressional delegate, Democrat Eleanor Holmes Norton, who has limited voting power on the House floor.

The Senate on February 26 passed a bill, 61–37, to add a House seat for the District of Columbia. The Senate voted for the bill after Nevada senator John Ensign, an opponent of gun control laws, got the Senate to agree to an amendment to the bill to repeal the District's ban on certain semi-automatic weapons, bar the city's registration requirements for most guns, and drop criminal penalties for possessing an unregistered firearm in the district.

The House planned to bring its own measure up for a vote in early March. But Democratic leaders postponed action on the bill after gun rights activists demanded that the measure include language to revise the city's gun laws. House Minority Leader John A. Boehner of Ohio said that Democratic leaders wanted to "deny Second Amendment rights to residents of our nation's capital."

House Majority Leader Steny H. Hoyer of Maryland said that repealing the gun laws would abrogate the "District's ability to manage its own laws."[44]

Delaying Transition from Analog to Digital TV

Obama on February 11 signed a bill to delay until June 12 the mandatory transition of television broadcasting from analog to digital.

The original deadline had been February 17, but the Obama administration had asked Congress for a delay because millions of Americans had not yet bought the special converter boxes that analog television users would need to continue watching free television signals on their sets. A $1.34 billion program to distribute $40 vouchers for the converter boxes had run out of money in January.

The Senate passed the bill on January 29 on an uncontested voice vote. The House on February 4 cleared the bill for Obama's signature on a vote of 264–158, with Democrats voting heavily in favor and Republicans voting heavily against the measure.

Science Policy

Another early goal of the Obama administration was to promote research on science. Obama, appearing before the National Academy of Sciences on April 27, noted that federal funding for the physical sciences had declined over the years and that schoolchildren in the United States continued to lag behind their foreign counterparts in math and science.

"A half century ago, this nation made a commitment to lead the world in scientific and technological innovation, to invest in education, in research, in engineering, to set a goal of reaching space and engaging every citizen in that historic mission," Obama said. "That was the high water mark of America's investment in research and development. And since then, our investments have steadily declined as a share of our national income. As a result, other countries are now beginning to pull ahead in the pursuit of this generation's great discoveries."

Obama said that his administration would spend at least 3 percent of its Gross Domestic Product (GDP) on "green" initiatives. He set a goal for the nation to reduce its carbon pollution by more than 80 percent by 2050. The president pledged to spend $150 billion over the next decade to promote renewable sources of energy. Other goals the president announced include increased funding for the National Institutes of Health and a multiyear plan to double funding for cancer research.

"Science is more essential for our prosperity, our security, our health, our environment, and our quality of life than it has ever been before," Obama said.

Swine Flu

At the end of his first 100 days, President Obama had to deal with a newly discovered influenza virus—known officially as the H1N1 flu but commonly referred to as "swine flu" because it was believed to have originated from pig farms in Mexico.

As of early June 2009, the Centers for Disease Control (CDC) had confirmed 13,217 cases of swine flu in all fifty states, the District of Columbia, and Puerto Rico. CDC reported twenty-seven deaths from that flu strain.

Obama asked the Congress for $1.5 billion in emergency funding to help monitor and track the virus and build the supply of antiviral drugs.

Senator Specter Switches Parties

Obama and his Democratic allies further strengthened their hand in the Senate when Pennsylvania senator Arlen Specter announced April 28 that he was changing his party affiliation from Republican to Democratic, thereby giving Democrats fifty-nine seats in the Senate to just forty for the Republicans.

Specter attributed his party switch in large part to his likely defeat in a Republican primary election in 2010 by Rep. Pat Toomey, a conservative former congressman (1999–2005) who had nearly defeated Specter in a 2004 primary. Specter had angered many Republicans with his critical vote in favor of President Obama's economic stimulus law.

"In the course of the last several months since the stimulus vote, I have traveled the state and surveyed the sentiments of the Republican Party in Pennsylvania and

Announcing a political triumph on his 100th day in office, Obama on April 29, 2009, holds a press conference welcoming Sen. Arlen Specter of Pennsylvania to the Democratic Party. Specter had said one day earlier that he was leaving the Republican Party and seeking reelection to the Senate in 2010 as a Democrat.

public opinion polls, observed other public opinion polls and have found that the prospects for winning a Republican primary are bleak," Specter said at a news conference on Capitol Hill.

Even as he said he would seek reelection in 2010 as a Democrat, Specter said that he would not be an automatic party-line vote for his new party's leadership.

"I will not be an automatic 60th vote," Specter said. He added: "If the Democratic Party asks too much, I will not hesitate to disagree and vote my independent thinking and what I consider as a matter of conscience to be in the interest of the state and nation."

President Obama and congressional Democrats hailed Specter's announcement, though they acknowledged that the famously independent Specter would not be a reflexive Democratic vote.

"I do think that having Arlen Specter in the Democratic caucus will liberate him to cooperate on critical issues, like health care, like infrastructure and job creation, areas where his inclinations were to work with us, but he was feeling pressure not to," Obama said on April 29.

Administration's Use of Technology

As Obama was announcing his new policies, he was using nontraditional methods of educating the public about them.

Obama did exceptionally well among younger voters in the 2008 campaign, in part because his campaign skillfully used social networking sites such as Facebook and MySpace to reach out to younger voters. It also used text-messaging and e-mail to solicit campaign contributions.

As president, Obama used some of his online campaign tools to promote his policies. The Obama administration revamped the White House Web site, www.whitehouse.gov, and became the first president to broadcast his weekly radio addresses on YouTube.

During the campaign, Obama could be seen frequently consulting his Blackberry, the personal e-mail device that has become ubiquitous in Washington, D.C. Though Presidents Clinton and Bush didn't e-mail during their presidencies, Obama came to an agreement with the Secret Service and other federal agencies that will allow the president to use a Blackberry to communicate with senior staff and some close friends.

White House press secretary Robert Gibbs said that Obama's Blackberry communications generally would be subject to the 1978 Presidential Records Act, which requires presidential administrations to document activities and policies of presidents. Some limited personal communications would be exempt from record-keeping, Gibbs said.

Obama sometimes employed some self-deprecating humor to illustrate his dependence on the Blackberry. A couple of weeks before he took office, and before he fashioned an agreement to use a Blackberry, Obama said that "they're going to pry it out of my hands."[45]

"In just the first few weeks, I've had to engage in some of the toughest diplomacy of my life. And that was just to keep my Blackberry," Obama joked at a black-tie dinner in Washington on January 31.

The White House sometimes would send out e-mail communications under Obama's name to promote political goals or legislative priorities. On February 2, after the House passed an economic stimulus bill, Obama sent an e-mail to his political supporters asking them for their "help to spread the word and build support" for the measure.

"It's not enough for this bill to simply pass Congress," Obama wrote. "Americans need to know how it will affect their lives—they need to know that help is on the way and that this administration is investing in economic growth and stability."

Right after Obama signed his economic recovery plan into law, his administration launched and promoted a new Web site, www.recovery.gov, to educate the American public about the provisions of the stimulus law and show how, when, and where the money will be spent.

Obama, in a speech to the National Conference of State Legislatures on March 20, said that his administration created the Web site "so that Americans can see where their tax dollars are going and make sure we're delivering results." He said that forty-six states

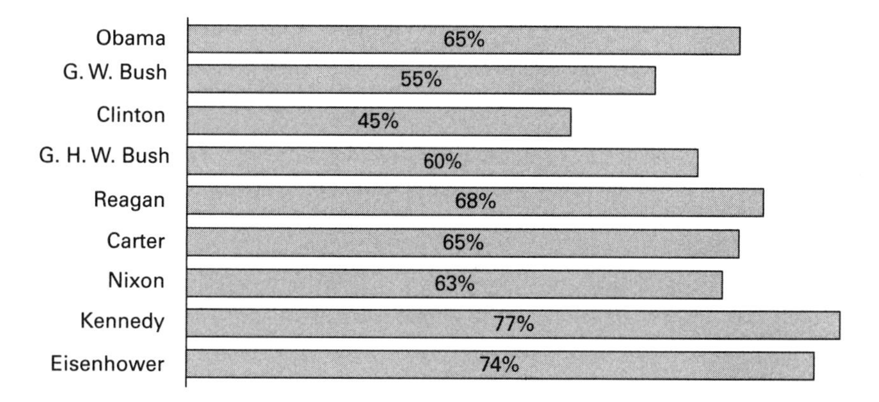

FIGURE 3
Comparison of Presidential Job Approval Averages after First 100 Days in Office

Source: Based on www.gallup.com/poll/118928/Obama-Approval-Compares-Favorably-Prior-Presidents.aspx.

had created Web sites that link to www.recovery.gov "to help people keep track of how money is being spent down to the local level."

Public Opinion at 100 Days

Media organizations and polling organizations conducted numerous surveys during Obama's first 100 days to gauge public impressions of his administration. And like recent past presidents, Obama's first 100 day were viewed more positively than negatively by the American people.

According to a compilation by the polling firm Clarus Research Group, Obama had an average approval rating of 63 percent over his first 100 days—higher than the 58 percent rating for George W. Bush and the 55 percent rating for Bill Clinton.

A *New York Times*–CBS survey conducted between April 22 and April 26 pegged Obama's approval rating at 68 percent and his disapproval rating at 27 percent. Seventy-two percent of respondents said that they were optimistic about the next four years with Obama as president, compared to 22 percent who said they were pessimistic.[46]

There were stark differences in public approval among self-identified Democrats, Republicans, and independents. A Gallup Poll taken from April 20 to April 26 found that 92 percent of Democratic respondents approved of Obama's job performance, compared to 64 percent of political independents and just 28 percent of self-identified Republicans.

Frank Newport, the editor in chief of the Gallup Poll, said that the 64-percentage-point gap between the Democratic and Republican approval ratings "is one of the bigger ones that we have seen in Gallup Poll history." "One of the reasons for that is that there are fewer Republicans now, our data show, and those that remain tend to be more conservative and therefore more likely to be negative about Barack Obama," Newport said.[47]

It's too early to tell if the American public will view the rest of Obama's first term as positively as they did his first 100 days in office. Some presidents who had higher approval ratings after 100 days in office were defeated for reelection four years later, while others were reelected.

How successful Obama is will depend on a variety of factors, not least the health of the national economy and how the public reacts to his policy agenda. At the end of his first 100 days, though, voters appeared to be giving Obama some leeway.

"Essentially, most voters either like what they see in Obama or are willing to give him a chance even if they have doubts," said Ron Faucheux, a political scientist and the president of Clarus Research Group. "The public's perception of his performance in office over the months ahead will determine how well or how long this situation holds up."

Notes

1. Gallup Polls available at www.gallup.com/poll/113980/Gallup-Daily-Obama-Job-Approval.aspx.
2. Michael E. Ruane and Aaron C. Davis, "D.C. Inauguration Head Count: 1.8 Million," *Washington Post*, January 22, 2009. Available at www.washingtonpost.com/wp-dyn/content/article/2009/01/21/AR2009012103884.html.
3. The transcript and video of Obama's inaugural address can be found at www.whitehouse.gov/blog/inaugural-address.
4. Article II, Section 1 of the U.S. Constitution. Available at www.archives.gov/exhibits/charters/constitution_transcript.html.
5. Senate Roll Call Vote 6, January 21, 2009. Available at www.senate.gov/legislative/LIS/roll_call_lists/roll_call_vote_cfm.cfm?congress=111&session=1&vote=00006.
6. Senate Roll Call Vote 32, February 2, 2009. Available at www.senate.gov/legislative/LIS/roll_call_lists/roll_call_vote_cfm.cfm?congress=111&session=1&vote=00032.
7. Jonathan Allen, "Gregg Voted to Kill Commerce before He Agreed to Lead It," *CQ Today*, February 2, 2009.
8. Adrienne Kroepsch, "Senate Confirms Locke as Commerce Secretary," *CQ Today*, March 24, 2009.
9. Rasmussen Reports survey taken January 18–19, 2009. Available at www.rasmussenreports.com/public_content/politics/obama_administration/january_2009/41_say_geithner_should_not_be_treasury_secretary.
10. Senate Roll Call Vote 15, January 26, 2009. Available at www.senate.gov/legislative/LIS/roll_call_lists/roll_call_vote_cfm.cfm?congress=111&session=1&vote=00015.
11. Drew Armstrong, "Daschle Withdraws over Tax Questions," *CQ Weekly*, 311.
12. Alex Wayne, "Sebelius Confirmed as Health and Human Services Secretary," *CQ Weekly*, May 4, 2009, 1043.
13. Senate Roll Call Vote 172, April 28, 2009. Available at www.senate.gov/legislative/LIS/roll_call_lists/roll_call_vote_cfm.cfm?congress=111&session=1&vote=00172.
14. Jonathan Allen and Karoun Demirjian, "Obama Chooses Rep. Solis for Labor Secretary," *CQ Today*, December 18, 2008.

15. Senate Roll Call Vote 66, February 24, 2009. Available at www.senate.gov/legislative/LIS/roll_call_lists/roll_call_vote_cfm.cfm?congress=111&session=1&vote=00066.
16. Tim Starks, "Panetta Confirmed by Voice Vote to Be CIA Director," *CQ Today,* February 12, 2009.
17. David Nather, "The Vice Presidency, According to Biden," *CQ Weekly,* April 6, 2009, 760.
18. Grassley letter available at www.politifact.com/media/files/GrassleyDocument.pdf.
19. Orszag/Craig letter available at www.politifact.com/media;/files/OrszagDocument.pdf.
20. Senate Roll Call Vote 62, February 11, 2009. Available at www.senate.gov/legislative/LIS/roll_call_lists/roll_call_vote_cfm.cfm?congress=111&session=1&vote=00062.
21. Josh Rogin, "With Lobbying Rules Waived, Lynn's Earlier Pentagon Tenure Now at Issue," *CQ Today,* January 23, 2009.
22. Adriel Bettelheim, "Obama Reverses Bush Policies," *CQ Weekly,* January 26, 2009, 184.
23. "'Mexico City' Policy's History," *CQ Weekly,* January 27, 2001, 236.
24. Adriel Bettelheim, "Obama Overturns Ban on Funds for Groups Supporting Overseas Abortion," *CQ Today,* Janaury 23, 2009.
25. National Right to Life Committee, January 23, 2009. Press release is available at www.nrlc.org/press_releases_new/Release012309.html.
26. Commerce Department release available at www.bea.gov/newsreleases/national/gdp/gdpnewsrelease.htm.
27. www.djindexes.com/DJIA110/learning-center.
28. House Roll Call Vote 46, January 28, 2009. Available at http://clerk.house.gov/evs/2009/roll046.xml.
29. John McCain floor speech, February 9, 2009.
30. President Obama's statement available at www.whitehouse.gov/the_press_office/StatementonRecoveryandReinvestmentActAgreement.
31. David Mercer, "Caterpillar CEO sees more company layoffs," The Associated Press, February 12, 2009. Available at http://finance.yahoo.com/news/Caterpillar-CEO-sees-more-apf-14347759.html.
32. CQ House Action Reports summary of conference agreement, February 13, 2009.
33. Senate Roll Call Vote 64, February 13, 2009. Available at www.senate.gov/legislative/LIS/roll_call_lists/roll_call_vote_cfm.cfm?congress=111&session=1&vote=00064.
34. Taxpayers for Common Sense research available at www.taxpayer.net.
35. Paul M. Krawzak and Kathleen Hunter, "Work Completed on '09 Omnibus," *CQ Weekly,* March 16, 2009, 612.
36. Senate Roll Call Vote 159, April 21, 2009. Available at www.senate.gov/legislative/LIS/roll_call_lists/roll_call_vote_cfm.cfm?congress=111&session=1&vote=00159.
37. Matthew Johnson, "Lawmakers Voice Bipartisan Support for Iraq Withdrawal Plans," *CQ Today Online News,* February 27, 2009.
38. Senate Roll Call Vote 14, January 22, 2009. Available at www.senate.gov/legislative/LIS/roll_call_lists/roll_call_vote_cfm.cfm?congress=111&session=1&vote=00014.
39. House Roll Call Vote 37, January 27, 2009. Available at http://clerk.house.gov/evs/2009/roll037.xml.
40. The Henry J. Kaiser Family Foundation, Kaiser Commission on Medicaid and the Uninsured, February 2009. Available at www.kff.org/medicaid/upload/7863.pdf.
41. Senate Roll Call Vote 31, January 29, 2009. Available at www.senate.gov/legislative/LIS/roll_call_lists/roll_call_vote_cfm.cfm?congress=111&session=1&vote=00031.
42. Memorandum to Energy Department available at www.whitehouse.gov/the_press_office/ApplianceEfficiencyStandards.
43. Lydia Gensheimer, "National Service Bill Aims to Draw on 'Very Best of the American People,'" *CQ Weekly,* March 30, 2009, 727.

44. Michael Teitelbaum, "Tussle Over Gun Language Delays House Action on D.C. Representative," *CQ Today,* March 3, 2009.
45. Jeff Zeleny, "Obama Digs In for His Blackberry," *The New York Times,* January 7, 2009. Available at www.nytimes.com/2009/01/08/us/politics/08berry.html.
46. The *New York Times*–CBS News Poll, April 22–26, 2009. Available at http://graphics8.nytimes.com/packages/images/nytint/docs/new-york-times-cbs-news-poll-obama-s-100th-day-in-office/original.pdf.
47. Newport's comments may be viewed at www.gallup.com/video/118048/Obama-Approval-100-Days.aspx.